The Curlew

Aesculus

The Curlew

Volume II Issue I

Aesculus

Published in 2017 by The Wild Wood Press, Caerwedros, Ceredigion, Wales, UK
www.the-curlew.com

ISBN 978 0 9550 1849 7

Edited by Dr Lynn Parr

Printed in Devon by Imprint Digital Ltd

Curlew logo drawn by Hester Cox, www.hestercox.com

Front cover: Llangrannog, Wales © Lynn Parr
Frontispiece: Horse Chestnut, *Aesculus hippocastanum*, Cumbria
© Lynn Parr

Contents

Bird Song

Classic Essay by John Burroughs

I suspect it requires a special gift of grace to enable one to hear the bird-songs; some new power must be added to the ear, or some obstruction removed. There are not only scales upon our eyes so that we do not see, there are scales upon our ears so that we do not hear.

A city woman who had spent much of her time in the country once asked a well-known ornithologist to take her where she could hear the bluebird. "What, never heard the bluebird!" said he. "I have not," said the woman. "Then you will never hear it," said the bird-lover; never hear it with that inward ear that gives beauty and meaning to the note. He could probably have taken her in a few minutes where she could have heard the call or warble of the bluebird; but it would have fallen upon unresponsive ears – upon ears that were not sensitized by love for the birds or associations with them.

Bird-songs are not music, properly speaking, but only suggestions of music. A great many people whose attention would be quickly arrested by the same volume of sound made by a musical instrument or by artificial means never hear them at all. The sound of a boy's penny whistle there in the grove or the meadow would separate itself more from the background of nature, and be a greater challenge to the ear, than is the strain of the thrush or the song of the sparrow. There is something elusive, indefinite, neutral, about bird-songs that makes them strike obliquely, as it were, upon the ear; and we are very apt to miss them. They are a part of nature, the Nature that lies about us, entirely occupied with her own affairs, and quite regardless of our presence. Hence it is with bird-songs as it is with so many other things in nature – they are what we make them; the ear that hears them must be half-creative.

I am always disturbed when persons not especially observant of birds ask me to take them where they can hear a particular bird, in whose song they have become interested through a description in some book. As I listen with them, I feel like apologizing for the bird: it has a bad cold, or has just heard some depressing news; it will not let itself out. The song seems so casual and minor when you make a dead set at it. I have taken persons to hear the hermit thrush, and I have fancied that they were all the time saying to themselves, "Is that all?" But should one hear the bird in his walk, when the mind is attuned to simple things and is open and receptive, when expectation is not aroused and the song comes as a surprise out of the dusky silence of the woods, then one feels that it merits all the fine things that can be said of it.

One of our popular writers and lecturers upon birds told me this incident: He had engaged to take two city girls out for a walk in the country, to teach them the names of the birds they might see and hear. Before they started, he read to them Henry van Dyke's poem on the song sparrow, telling them that the song sparrow was one of the first birds they were likely to hear. As they proceeded with their walk, sure enough, there by the roadside was a sparrow in song. The bird man called the attention of his companions to it. It was some time before the unpracticed ears of the girls could make it out; then one of them said (the poem she had just heard, I suppose, still ringing in her ears), "What! That little squeaky thing?" The sparrow's song meant nothing to her at all, and how could she share the enthusiasm of the poet? Probably the warble of the robin, or the call of the meadowlark, if they chanced to hear them, meant no more to these girls.

If we have no associations with these sounds, they will mean very little to us. Their merit as musical performances is very slight. It is as signs of joy and love in nature, as heralds of spring, and as the spirit of the woods and fields made audible, that they appeal to us. The drumming of the woodpeckers and of the ruffed grouse give great pleasure to a countryman, though these sounds have not the quality of real music. It is the same with the call of the migrating geese or the voice of any wild thing: our pleasure in them is entirely apart from any considerations of music. Why does the wild flower, as we chance upon it in the woods or bogs, give us more pleasure than the more elaborate flower of the garden or lawn? Because it comes as a surprise, offers a greater contrast with its surroundings, and suggests a spirit in wild nature that seems to take thought of itself and to aspire to beautiful forms.

Many years ago some skylarks were liberated on Long Island, and they became established there, and may now occasionally be heard in certain localities. One summer day a friend of mine was out there observing them; a lark was soaring and singing in the sky above him. An old Irishman came along, and suddenly stopped as if transfixed to the spot; a look of mingled delight and incredulity came into his face. Was he indeed hearing the bird of his youth? He took off his hat, turned his face skyward, and with moving lips and streaming eyes stood a long time regarding the bird. "Ah," my friend thought, "if I could only hear that song with his ears!" How it brought back his youth and all those long-gone days on his native hills!

The power of bird-songs over us is so much a matter of association that every traveller to other countries finds the feathered songsters of less merit than those he left behind. The stranger does not hear the birds in the same receptive, uncritical frame of mind as does the native; they are not in the same way the voices of the place and the season. What music can there be in that long, piercing, far-heard note of the first meadowlark in spring to any but a native, or in the "o-ka-lee" of the red-shouldered starling as he rests upon the willows in March? A stranger would probably recognize melody and a wild woodsy quality in the flutings of the veery thrush; but how much more they would mean to him after he had spent many successive Junes threading our northern trout-streams and encamping on their banks! The veery will come early in the morning, and again at sundown, and perch above your tent, and blow his soft, reverberant note for many minutes at a time. The strain repeats the echoes of the limpid stream in the halls and corridors of the leafy woods.

While in England in 1882, I rushed about two or three counties in late June and early July, bent on hearing the song of the nightingale, but missed it by a few days, and in some cases, as it seemed, only by a few hours. The nightingale seems to be wound up to go only so long, or till about the middle of June, and it is only by a rare chance that you hear one after that date. Then I came home to hear a nightingale in song one winter morning in a friend's house in the city. It was a curious let-down to my enthusiasm. A caged song in a city chamber in broad daylight, in lieu of the wild, free song in the gloaming of an English landscape! I closed my eyes, abstracted myself from my surroundings, and tried my best to fancy myself listening to the strain back there amid the scenes I had haunted about Haslemere and Godalming, but with poor success, I suspect. The nightingale's song, like the lark's, needs vista, needs all the accessories of time and place. The song is not all in the singing, any more than the wit is all in the saying. It is in the occasion, the surroundings, the spirit of which it is the expression. My friend said that the bird did not fully let itself out. Its song was a brilliant medley of notes – no theme that I could detect – like the lark's song in this respect; all the notes of the field and forest appeared to be the gift of this bird, but what tone! what accent! like that of a great poet!

A very interesting feature of our bird-songs is the wing-song, or song of ecstasy. It is not the gift of many of our birds. Indeed, less than a dozen species are known to me as ever singing on the wing. It seems to spring from more intense excitement and self-abandonment than the ordinary song delivered from the perch. When its joy reaches the point of rapture, the bird is literally carried off its feet, and up it goes into the air, pouring out its song as a rocket pours out its sparks.

Probably the perch-songster among our ordinary birds that is most regularly seized with the fit of ecstasy that results in this lyric burst in the air, as I described in my first book, *Wake Robin*, over thirty years ago, is the oven-bird, or wood-accentor – the golden-crowned thrush of the old ornithologists. Every loiterer about the woods knows this pretty, speckled-breasted, olive-backed little bird, which walks along over the dry leaves a few yards from him, moving its head as it walks, like a miniature domestic fowl. Most birds are very stiff-necked, like the robin, and as they run or hop upon the ground, carry the head as if it were riveted to the body. Not so the oven-bird, or the other birds that walk, as the cow-bunting, or the quail, or the crow. They move the head forward with the movement of the feet. The sharp, reiterated, almost screeching song of the oven-bird, as it perches on a limb a few feet from the ground, like the words, "preacher, preacher, preacher," or "teacher, teacher, teacher," uttered louder and louder, and repeated six or seven times, is also familiar to most ears; but its wild, ringing, rapturous burst of song in the air high above the tree-tops is not so well known. From a very prosy, tiresome, unmelodious singer, it is suddenly transformed for a brief moment into a lyric poet of great power. It is a great surprise. The bird undergoes a complete transformation.

Ordinarily it is a very quiet, demure sort of bird. It walks about over the leaves, moving its head like a little hen; then perches on a limb a few feet from the ground and sends forth its shrill, rather prosy, unmusical chant. Surely it is an ordinary, common-place bird. But wait till the inspiration of its flight-song is upon it. What a change! Up it goes through the branches of the trees, leaping from limb to limb, faster and faster, till it shoots from the tree-tops fifty or more feet into the air above them, and bursts into an ecstasy of song, rapid, ringing, lyrical; no more like its habitual performance than a match is like a rocket; brief but thrilling; emphatic but musical. Having reached its climax of flight and song, the bird closes its wings and drops nearly perpendicularly downward like the skylark. If its song were more prolonged, it would rival the song of that famous bird. The bird does this many times a day during early June, but oftenest at twilight. The song in quality and general cast is like that of its congener, the water-accentor, which, however, I believe is never delivered on the wing. From its habit of singing at twilight, and from the swift, darting motions of the bird, I am inclined to think that in it we have solved the mystery of Thoreau's "night-warbler," that puzzled and eluded him for years. Emerson told him he must beware of finding and booking it, lest life should have nothing more to show him.

Blackbird

Lynne Caddick

In the rain-soaked garden, a blackbird sings:
music in the greenness. Two notes slide into one
bell beak rung out with insistent vigour. Spring clear,
even paced and without fatigue.
To whom does he sing?

In the cloisters of eucalyptus and rose
I am aware of his song-filled presence, my senses
cross the threshold of his greenly garden space.
Singly he sings. His morning song is rain and dew.
Gulls glide beyond slate and stack, swoop

down to drag me into vastness; fish slide
through green water; a cat walks silently,
nimbly across a wall; the heron waits.
Even here, where the telos is death,
the bird-beak song sings out its joy.

Squaring the Circle

Finola Scott

They promise polar bears.
For days we head up, beyond
the tree line, to the white of the globe,
where flags and sledges hide.

In constant light we haunt the rails.
Whales cruise past spouting carefree,
but no polar bears. The ice field's not
where it should be. Its melting edge slips
in summer's heat. Sapphire glaciers shift.

So this crystal morning, tannoys haul
dreamers from cabin to empty deck,
hard-core naturalists separate from tourists.
The dedicated don't pause to dress.

We scan bobbing ice floes and remember
ice-cream floats in cafés. Then walrus!
Blancmange blobs heave onto ice, lumber,
roar and snort. Mothers loll, blubbery
babies big as cows practise skidding.
They slide and wobble over aquamarine.

Held by the curve of the Arctic, in pyjamas
and cardies, we peer sleepy-eyed. Careless
of cold we wonder at this beauty served up
in longitude and latitude slices of pie.

Saved by the Bear

Cliff Wright

Pedal Power

Pat Edwards

Biking my bones along the canal tow path,
another toppled tree reflected in still water,
makes me pedal that little bit harder.
After all, if the wind can do that to a tree,
and the water can dissolve it day by day,
what can breathing in and out do to me.

My feeble tissue is made of the same carbon,
and my body is a mass of watery exchanges.
If I pedal that little bit harder, I can chase
down the wind and get ahead, get ahead.
Look, I am the gilded air and the dragonfly,
the fleeting moments in my own tow path.

So

Alison Brackenbury

So in my dream the birds were bats.

There is that chill which shocks the spine
as daylight thickens, as the line
which flashes over lane or street
is not a bird, which drops to eat
on tables at your garden's end,
which may have names, familiar, friend.
It is a bat, with needled teeth,
which lets the last blue tilt beneath
at dizzy speed, not needing light
as badger, hedgehog tunnel night
without their eyes, see sound, hear scents,
but bats are speed. A bat has leant
on windless air, flicked body clean,
before eye slows all it has seen,
poised in the gap from warmth to words.

But when I woke, the bats were birds.

Murmuration

Rachel Burns

The sky a reddening hue
and then the murmuration
starlings blacking out the sky
blotting out the hum drum
of the small redbrick housing estate
continuing over the high security prison
over the drab grey walls.
The sound continuing, settling
down by dusk
as if they are saying
this world belongs to us.

Ballantrae in its Heyday

Maggie Mackay

On a quiet bay, Baile na Tràgha on the Carrick coast,
on the River Stinchar's tidal pools,
a place of excellent salmon beats and trout fishing.
Shingle-sand lapping Ailsa Craig, Arran and Kintyre.
Sky thick with offshore divers, Manx shearwaters, gannets.
Harbour crowded by barrels of white herrings, beside cod, ling, and hake,
fish-curers' song, coopers' hammers,
boat pitch by stone-worn jetty.
Noted as a smugglers' haunt, a rude and primitive
place of brandy and revolutionary ideas hefted into rocky coves,
hill tenant shepherds blown ruddy with sea salt in their beards.

Light on the Estuary

Featured Artist Jonathan Trim

Incoming Tide

Grey Day in the Estuary

Summer Gorse on Two Tree Island

Evening on Two Tree Island

Ebb Tide Late Afternoon

Low Tide and a Curlew Calls

Evening

Kitty Coles

The evening is blue as a vein
and tremulous, stirring,
full-bellied with the weight of water.

Leaves rearrange themselves
incessantly. They tessellate
the paths with their red and yellow.

This white branch
of the birch is bearded with cobweb.
Its skin is leprous, peeling under my fingers.

The geese fly low, calling discordantly.
The undersides of their wings
are coloured like mushrooms.

The water darkens. Near its centre,
a gull is floating, a blur of silence,
dematerialising.

Hike over Raccoon Ridge

David Crews

Climbing the AT ridge
toward the Gap
kestrels arrive early
before prairie warblers
great-crested flycatchers
indigo buntings.
An eagle rides the thermals
tight gyres overhead
that disappear into bright
haze of afternoon. The woods
in winter you say
all gray matter
a holding pattern
seeming stillness
of skeleton trees and leaves
scattered throughout the forest
but here in the heart of April
life again springs forth
below in the valley
ferns push through
leaf litter, webs of violet
crawl in and out and over
rockbeds and high
on Raccoon Ridge
in the unbloomed
mountain laurel field sparrows
sing crescendos into vistas
stretching far horizons
these poems, these
songs.

Wild Encounters

Cliff Wright

Nature complies. The first time I remember it happening I was around five years old. "Your son," my teacher told my mother, "is going to be an artist." Her conviction, prophetic as it transpired, was based upon an exercise whereby our class had been asked to draw a fox. My attempt, apparently, was the only one that didn't look like a box. Perhaps, I hear you say, I had the best hearing? That aside, what the teacher failed to notice was that the episode also signalled a growing passion for all things wild and foxes in particular.

Very many years later, halfway through the day, I was feeling rather hungry. Busily painting my current commission, I was loathe to find the time for a lunch break when a small but insistent voice whispered inside my head. "Just have one apple," it instructed. "Go and eat it under the apple tree and ten minutes after a fox will trot past. Oh, and never worry, the fox won't see you."

I haven't always listened to that voice, but on this golden occasion I did as beckoned – and to the minute and my delight, a fox duly obliged – it passed so close I could hear its footfall, but it paid no attention to me. It was as though I was invisible. By the way, I'm responsible, along with all due credit to my mum, for that tree. She repeatedly imparted her certain knowledge that if I threw my apple cores over the fence, a tree would one day grow there. Of course I believed her unquestioningly, religiously discarding half-eaten apples, and nature – magically to me, anyway – complied. Our apple tree has returned many more fruits to us than

© Cliff Wright

ever I disposed of; feeding us, the rodents, insects, slugs, worms, birds, badgers and foxes. I'm very grateful to it, and to my mum. More about the tree, and Mum, later...

© Cliff Wright

So I was blessed with what I remember as a childhood well-suited to one who appreciated the freedom to roam over a large (to me then, small to me now) area of nature, shared, apart from the occasional dog-walker, only with wild creatures. At this young age, encounters with the wildlife were, as I recall, rare and fleeting and although I was aware of them and they must certainly have been of me crashing through the brambles, we were not yet connecting. But I was never happier than when spending many hours exploring trails or making my own through tangled undergrowth or making camps and places to hide in. One thing leaps out to me as a clear and vivid memory. I used to tell myself with total conviction that if I walked through a bed of nettles barefoot, whilst believing that they would not sting, I would escape unscathed. And yes, nature again complied.

My father was the first to shatter the idyll when, 27 years ago following a year of treatment for a heart condition and subsequent heart attack, he suddenly left us. We are a close family and although different in many ways, we have a very strong core of love at our centre. Mum is the centre and she was devastated, knowing for certain that she had lost her one and only love.

My sister and I gathered ourselves for Mum and she for us by the steadfast way she dealt with the unimaginable change to our world. Sherlock Holmes once said, "Work is the best antidote to sorrow." I retreated into my painting and creation of children's books and of course it helped that the foxes were still calling nearby and nature was on the doorstep. I have lived with Mum ever since – until now.

Recurring dreams are fascinating things. Something in me believes that they will keep recurring until we explore or discover their messages. I have had one such which always leaves me feeling joyful and complete. Peopled by various animals, and with countless variations of story, the essence of the dream is, however, always the

© Cliff Wright

same: I am closely connecting, sometimes even communicating with, wild animals. The process is effortless and feels as natural as breathing.

Fifteen or so years ago I followed the dream and found myself on a wilderness awareness course in the USA. Taught by Tom Brown, a tracker who had been raised by a Native American elder, I arrived nervously and left reluctantly after a week feeling as though I had met another, very ancient, family. This was my first introduction to meditation and was an overwhelming confirmation that deep nature connection is not only possible but fundamentally necessary. I learned so many things which, although new, felt like distant memories – how to see with wide vision, how to slow down and walk like a fox, and so on.

On fire with the desire to practise my re-found abilities, upon returning home I eagerly trod my first trail. Within a few yards, to my utter surprise, I walked straight up to a sleeping fox (I nearly stepped on it), hitherto hidden in long grass. I was invisible again! To my delight (I would have been very disappointed if it had been otherwise), I also managed to retreat without waking the fox.

Nature complies. And so begins my closest encounter so far.

Two years ago at the end of May, I am sitting underneath our apple tree for my usual evening meditation. It is almost dark and dim at best under the tree. Small rustlings betray the presence of other creatures and finally draw my attention as they turn into dark forms, coming closer. Rabbits? No, a little larger. Closer still – fox cubs? Yes! Four of them, tiny and just a yard or two in front of me, carefully, inquisitively, exploring; seemingly unaware of me. In the darkness it feels as though it's their first time with the tree, new smells, new sensations – their mum must be nearby. I sit very still, my mind empty. Now they move, now they creep, dart, play, sit, jump and run. At last they melt away and my thinking mind returns – did that just happen?

Subsequent evenings reveal that it wasn't a dream. The four cubs appear regularly, and by gradual turns become bolder and braver. I follow their lead and sit out every night, same time. At such a young age fox cubs are as curious as they are wary and haven't yet learned all the things they should be scared of. They also love peanuts, I discover. I wonder about feeding wild creatures as I don't want to encourage dependence. On the other hand, it's a tough existence out there in nature and foxes have been unfairly persecuted for far too long. I prefer the Native American view that we are the guardians of nature. So a handful of peanuts scattered in the grass seems OK. The foxes think so, too, and they are happy with my presence, yet also wonderfully and reassuringly easily spooked. As the encounters increase and their courage multiplies, the boldest is brave enough to take a nut from my hand – though the movement of my finger, even by a millimetre, will elicit a very rapid retreat or the most comical and intense attention, and the occasional nip. Fox cub teeth, I find out, are as sharp as needles. Their claws, too, would give the sharpest pins a run for their money as they kindly reveal to me when the first one climbs onto my hand.

Not to be outdone, one by one the other cubs learn from their brave sibling and I am blessed by close contact with each of them. Characters begin to emerge in front of me as the individuals begin to assert themselves – such a privilege to witness. One is smaller and is the shyest – I guess she is the female. She and her brothers are clearly finding their feet and sorting out who is who, and just the same as humans – this varies as the mood takes. Sometimes but rarely, mum appears too. Two or three times she suckles her offspring just in front of me. On another occasion she walks right past me carrying a large pheasant – the excitement of the cubs over this present is just out of sight, but clearly audible. Foxes make the most incredible variety of sounds, all with their own meaning, but the vixen's scream, heard from a few inches away, is impressive indeed!

Memorably, one evening a cub is in my lap trying to find the hidden nuts in the folds of my coat when I hear a badger approaching. For once, my ears are in advance of the fox, but at the last minute he realises, jumps out of my lap and flattens himself to the ground like a rug, just in time for the badger to wander past, oblivious to the crouching fox mere inches away.

I should mention here that I'm also on good terms with a female badger that I've known for over three years. She is one of the most intelligent animals (including dogs) that I have had the pleasure to be acquainted with, and quickly solves any challenges that I cannot resist putting her way. Her appearances are less regular than the foxes but she has also learnt to trust enough to climb onto me in search of peanuts. Badgers are very much heavier than foxes!

Sometimes fox and badger will turn up at the same time. As you may guess, usually the badger dominates, but it isn't always the case. If the fox is feeling particularly belligerent and the badger uncertain, she will give way.

Over months the three male fox cubs slowly give me less attention until one by one they disperse, as is their wont. The shy female stays and visits almost every night if she is within earshot, appearing minutes after I whistle 'Amazing Grace'. She is very comfortable with me as long as she is allowed to observe her chosen rituals: First approach and retreat, then approach closer, then climb onto my lap. One evening I happen to hesitate for a moment in releasing a peanut and instantly she touches her nose to mine. I quickly work out that this is the signal for the next nut –

I am honoured indeed and it becomes another ritual.

Suddenly, a large area of scrub nearby is cleared without warning by someone claiming that he has bought the land. The affect on the foxes is devastating. The mum disappears, never to reappear, and the following night I see the one remaining cub wandering over the cleared space searching for somewhere to bury a cache. She eventually chooses a mound of loose earth which I am certain is the destroyed sett. We have no idea of the impact of our actions.

And what of those times when the fox doesn't show up? Or those times when I have to go away for a few days? Human minds are remarkable things. We can work out the most complex problems and decide this and that, but we jump to conclusions and judge good and bad so quickly. It is so easy to become attached to wild encounters and to claim their results.

I find myself watching my mind leaping to thoughts of: "What if something has happened to her?" or "Perhaps she is injured, or even dead". But of course I know this animal for just a few minutes of its day; a snapshot into its life. A very privileged insight, it is true, but I simply don't have the big picture – which of us ever does? So I return to stillness of the mind and meditation and there is space again for anything to be true. And sometimes after a hiatus from our encounters, I'll get an inkling that tonight she will turn up again.

And nature mysteriously complies.

My mum's turn to change the picture came this year in the middle of March. Having been the fittest of 81-year-olds, to our utter disbelief she contracted a terminal leukemia and was given just a few months. The rapid progression of the disease led to my sister and myself caring for her 24/7 and we were privileged (because we absolutely knew what Mum wanted) to be able to shower her with love all the while in her own home. She passed on the 8th of October and knew how much she was loved. It is such an profound event to lose a parent, especially the second one. The sense of loss is overwhelming, the grief at times unbearable, albeit interspersed with moments of extreme gratitude for the preciousness of life.

I recalled my fox cub, who had also lost her mum and who I was so very fortunate to encounter every night of my mum's illness.

Our little area of wild land is not so slowly but now very surely being consumed by housing developments and land-grabbing. The inevitability of it is hard to accept having grown up alongside a tree that I planted as a young boy and a wilderness that I have had so many magical adventures with over so many years. I am enriched and spoilt by the experience so it looks like it may be time to move on.

The archaeology that preceded the first of the housing estates revealed our hillside to be one of the oldest inhabited parts of Sussex. On the surface of the land that we see now, all trace of those inhabitants would be hard to see. But it occurs to me that those earliest of dwellers would have had foxes, badgers and others such as bears for company, should they have had the eyes to see them. In hundreds of years will our rapidly built housing have outlasted the wildlife?

There is solace in the knowledge that nature endures, but the bears are now long gone, and really, we could be doing a much better job of caring for our wildlife, loving it even, while we are here. A fox is not just another fox, a badger not just another badger. They are as individual as people and just as moody. They don't have the luxuries of heating and lighting and solid walls and they don't need them, but they would benefit enormously from our care, as would we. It is remarkable to me that, given our general and great ignorance of their lives, wild creatures adapt and survive so well right under our very noses. We all originate from the same source; damage one element of that source and we damage ourselves.

I teach drawing-based workshops. The secret to drawing is to see beyond that which you think you know. Once this 'real' seeing happens the quality of the drawing improves and the experience is life-affirming. It is exactly the same thing as connecting with nature and the ability to access it is within us all. Is it any accident that on my courses those who can let go of their ideas the most, who care and love the most, also see more wildlife?

Nature always complies. Thank you to my family, to the hillside, to the tree and to the wildlife.

© *Cliff Wright*

Waste Not, Want Not

Aziz Dixon

I am an eco-warrior,
one of the town vigilantes.
All our gang have fine pink feet.
Our mission is to stop the waste –
so much food would be lost
without us, but they do not understand,
these crazy bipeds.

I have my own patch to patrol –
not the seafront for me.
There's a bus shelter right outside
the upmarket chip shop, and often
I can catch their eye,
when they're enjoying a meal.
Anything not eaten, and
I'll yodel all across town
(I'm proud of my yodelling, actually.)
Then
we'll swoop in the street
on the unsuspecting, the gull-ible,
seizing chips, sampling
the cod in batter (on a good day) –
just to teach them a lesson.
First done, help the others,
as my Granddad used to say.

On Walking to Fleet Church

Tee Francis

We trod the ancient coastal path
warm-baked on an April Sunday,
felt the thud of our feet lay down
the desk-bound work of a digital week,
swung the wind-worn kissing gate.
The Fleet stretched out its long sand arm;
held us close in the glistening heat.

Oyster catchers, egrets and terns
stalked the lagoon of Chesil Beach
while we turned driftwood, shells and thoughts.
In peace we walked to the small stone church,
ushered in by field-spun larks; the grassland
laced with fritillaries and bees,
we communed in the blessing of this day
exhaled our praise into the breeze.

Badger on the Boyne

Jane Burn

I sail to catch the Prince of the river,
nestled in willow, bobbed in hide, trawling
for salmon to eat myself wise. Come to my hook,
thou pretty silver fish! His shape, tempting-slick
under boat skin – I have spent my life wishing
on mouthfuls of hazelnut. Just one lick
of your shining sides is all I need, I swear.
Then I shall be King of all Creatures!
Great FinTan, if I cannot eat you then perhaps
you can spare a kiss? I will keep my teeth
behind my lips, promise I will not bite.
Not a nip of your sweet sushi sides! If only
I could know what you know! I would use it
for good, would rule with velvet paws.
I would be kind. My coracle would be solid gold,
reflecting sun in its cup as I bask, furry and royal
in sable skin, a diamond crown put rakish
on my skull, for how should I be king
without one, eh? Voles on the banks
shall worship as I pass – I shall keep a harem
of birds above my head. They shall sing
my passing in proclamations of squawk.
Bow down! Here sails the majesty of all
our Earth – benevolence in ev'ry hair! Behold!
For he carries the mark of angels striped
upon his head! That slick – he turns
his eyeballs from the deep and laughs
at my grandiose ideal, bubbles like balls of glass.
I will get your wisdom yet! I shake my fist.
It is just a matter of widening my net.

Squirrel Tales

Steve Harrison

Another maligned grey import
curio of landowners to scuttle among the Rhododendron
or scramble head first down the Cypress trees.
    Fast or nimble
head popping in different places
    in Heisenberg uncertainty.

What ever happened to Tufty?
Toggled up in waistcoat
    pushed out like Celts to the fringes
or boy scouts ferried to Brownsea Island
surviving on the edges of the branches;
Pine martin your new ally.
    Survival of the fattest
Over sexed and Over here.
    YouTube Star of Mission Impossible soundtracks
and acrobatics.
Like Yanks in War Time
bushy tailed
    back flipping at the hop to impress the local ladies.

Unseen circus act of suburban gardens,
I see the shells smashed open on the concrete mushroom,
    I hear a swish in the almond tree
too late to spot the dare devil   of the empty trapeze.

with acknowledgement to Philip Gross for a conversation about squirrels and sub-atomic particles

Water Rails

Audrey Ardern-Jones

slate blue heads sifting through reed banks
sliced smiles on red bills
impatient, jabbing frozen ground,

loose skirts of white on white
breathless, cold;

amidst low flying herons
fan-winged bitterns and tufted ducks

unaware of malicious intent;

enigmatic, tiptoeing claws
like enemies, duplicitous, difficult to spot.

The Stillness of Birds

Featured Artist Deborah Vass

Lapwing

Starling

Rook

Cormorant

Heron

An Intentional Gardener

Featured Poet Carolyn Martin

Arrival

This week spring
smuggled passels
of squills and crocuses
into our yard.
Which means
it's clear-out time
for weeds and moss
and all those broken twigs
sticking to the bottom
of the pond.

But a poem is chasing
me around the house –
its inconvenient voice
fending off practicalities,
demanding attention
for nothing more
than ornament.

When has a sonnet
pruned a fir?
A quatrain
thatched a lawn?
And free verse?
Not sharp enough
to root out
rotten stumps
or relocate a bush.

Today I'll negotiate
how deep
I'll have to dig
to find words
to cultivate.
Poems aggravate
that way.

Shall I Compare Thee to a Summer's Day?

I better not. You'd boil at the thought.
Might I entice you toward an early spring?
You could explode through thaw like daffodils
or strut with stellar jays around our yard.
Or, how about the star magnolia tree
that beats out cherry, plum, forsythia
each year and risks a frost to be the first?
Something in you, my dear, desires to lead,
can't bear the thought of standing second-best.

But let me clarify: there's just no way
you are the mower needing sharpening
nor peat that rests behind our garden shed
nor surly rains that shut a gardener in.
You've gleaned – withstanding twenty years
of partnering – I am the mower dulled
from summer's wear. I am the peat that waits
its spread as soon as coastal storms abate.
And, if you wish, I'd even be the shed.
Something in me feels worthy to protect.

But if these images still needle you
and you'd prefer the echo of a smile,
organic food consuming kitchen shelves,
the copper tint you splashed across our walls,
please humor me. Jot down on sticky notes
the things that speak to you of you. Arrange
them like perennials in tidy rows
near my writing pad and coffee cup.
I am an unlined page and cooling brew.

Through the Lifting Morning Fog

There – across the yard where mums bloom burgundy,
between the maple and hinoki trees –
a spider web sixty circles wide tethered
in a splint of light. If my body tilts
a bit or my glance angles toward the sky,
it disappears. This artistry demands
straight-on sight and backdrops of evergreens
to confirm it exists. So I stand still –
ignoring the cat sniffing candy tufts,
snubbing red leaves curled on the patio –
captured by the quiddity of silk,
free to ponder how, my dear, we connect
like single threads spiraling/winding/spun.
Whatever backdrops we appropriate,
we're content, it seems, with today's design,
angling to re-weave tomorrow's dawn, bound
by silken lines, by faith our tethers hold.

A Sonnet for Plotting Amateurs

Deep Pink, the package claimed and photographed
our dream of gladiola sprays. We mapped
three dozen bulbs around our pastel plots
as complements, we thought, to bright-eyed phlox,
petunias, asters, salvia and mums
and contrasts to the brooding firs we'd come
to love. But amateurs miss facts: bees
are un-enamored of this color scheme
and weak-kneed hummingbirds whir by
thumbing wings at pinks and blues and whites.
We'd only half a natural world until
some mischief rescued our design. It filled
our yard with orange glads in mid-July,
then shrugged with birds and bees, *So labels lie.*

A Requiem in November

They hadn't given up. Last night they thumbed
their stems at nasty wind and rain
and scooted south to hide in soggy grass.

This morning they held their colors fast,
clinging to gloves, boots, and rakes, begging for
a stab at life for another day.

What do you do when sugar maples' reds
and yellow-oranges make you want to cry?
When short-lived intensity asks for help?

You could decoupage the yard, then melt
blocks of paraffin and dip hangers-on
on every lichened limb. You could explain

it's nothing personal. Point out basil,
begonias, coleus ripped by frost.
You could concede that Nature is unkind

when your valley's snow rarely falls below
five hundred feet and nothing you prescribe
can relieve months of gray. A last resort,

you could rake a pyre and jump spread-eagled
into its multi-colored heart, bearing
witness to each leaf as it crisps and fades.

Storm Advisory

A winter storm makes land at dawn.
Surging seas. Valley snow down
to 100 feet. Schools already closed.

Here's to one more day before brutal snow
shuts my garden down and sends me fireside.
Time, at last, to thaw out tired limbs and doze
without bark slivers in my hands or dirt
beneath my fingernails. I've grown weary
of the earth I've kneaded daily with intent.
From spring to early frost, perennials
fulfilled their promises and, without pause,
bulbs splashed colors on my plotted beds.
Now I'm done with mudding through autumn rain –
saving diehard blooms, erasing moss and weeds –
exhausted by the beauty I conceived.

And, yet... I've come to know myself enough
to know I'll fret for phlox and bleeding hearts,
for jasmine climbing up the backyard fence;
for hostas, dahlias, daisies, roses, mums;
for everything I've grown to love. Before
daylight winds down and solar lights go dark,
I have it in me to push fatigue aside –
to prune, mulch, rake, embrace one more
bedding down, one irreparable goodbye.
Then, let smirking clouds cascade from the coast
and dawn reap relentless snow.
I'll design next spring out of winter sleep.

Snowfox

Fred Montague

Painted Leaves

Ram Nag

The tree stands nude –
A mute victim
Of the crimes of man.
Stripped bare
And its limbs hacked,
Its body gleams
With painted leaves.
If you maim a man
And give him crutches
Does that make you
A good Samaritan?
Like a murderer
Placing flowers
At his victim's grave
We have painted leaves
On its barren trunk.
Is it guilt?
Or is it a sadist's scheme
To remind the tree
Of its tremendous loss
For ages to come?

This poem is a response to a modern trend in India –
to cut down trees then paint them with leaves.

Edgelands of Tiddesley Woods

Holly-Elizabeth Toney

Patchwork quilts of verdant pasture, pastel blue skies a mesmerising backdrop to the swooping melody of passing nightingales; a quiet escape where wilderness is abundant. Such bucolic idylls are what many of us think of when imagining rural landscapes in England. Although rose-tinted, it is clear to see why many think in such a way. As we go about our everyday lives, we are blind to the reality which awaits us. One minute, we are traversing bustling cities and nearby towns and the next, narrow lanes lead us into a rapid change of scenery consisting of endless meadows and wooded hollows. Very few notice that there is not just a sudden shift between urban and rural landscapes. Instead, they are carefully drawn out until they meld and intertwine. Over time, this becomes part of the rural-urban edge, and the two dissimilar archetypes begin to negotiate and renegotiate their borders in the silent fringes of society until one outweighs the other. These are our edgelands, where nature enthrals itself in human disregard, including itself in bursts of scrublands and ruderal plants within the unnatural scarring left by waste and forgotten memories.

Edgelands, though a combination of two elements which are regularly traversed, are not meant to be seen. If they are, it is only by chance. They're the blurry backdrops to our car journeys as we look out of the passenger seat window, though even this does not enthral us enough into caring about such an environment. More to the point, it seems, is that nobody wants to see them. We pretend that they do not exist, with some believing they tarnish our natural countryside, and so we rush between urban and rural landscapes in the hopes of forgetting their existence. But with this ignorance comes missed opportunities. Rusted gates may hang off their hinges, their perforated edges inciting scares of tetanus, but what lies beyond them could enter the realms of endless possibilities and mystery.

I had never truly experienced this concept of edgelands until I was at least ten. I didn't begin to truly understand them, though, until I was in my early twenties. Spending the entirety of my youth nestled in the comfort of agricultural pasture surrounding my house and the adjacent village, alongside the market town of Pershore where I lived in Worcestershire, the idea of a rural-urban No Man's Land didn't even exist. Rural life seemingly came to a dead end once it began its interactions with its urban counterpart, one taking over where the other left off. It felt as though the notion of edgelands had been concealed from the public's very knowledge; if you wanted to find out the truth for yourself, you had to go out and find it. It was only then, at ten years old, that I ventured out of my comfort zone and stepped onto the fringes of town.

As most weekends would begin in our household, my mother and I took the simple pleasures of countryside walks into our stride. We would take in all the myriad smells and sights as we fumbled through wakes of fields and peat bogs, from the sweet tang of cow manure in the summer heat to the distant makeshift framework of heath on the summits of the Malvern Hills. The journeys could be intense, but we yearned for adventure. That was when we stumbled upon Tiddesley Woods.

Ebbing away from civilisation, the woods have provided a natural backdrop to the town for hundreds of years. Their versatility is noted on information boards placed around the wood's entrances, with facts and figures outlined to keep people absorbed in the once primeval forest that covered miles of uninhabited land. This semi-natural ancient woodland has existed since the last ice sheets retreated over 6,000 years ago, bringing with it successive waves of animals and insects to live in its diverse range of habitats. Even during this prehistory, though, humans had denuded the tree cover significantly with their urgency for farm and grazing land for their cattle and ever-growing businesses. Though they once bordered onto the town itself, the woods now only stand at around 65 hectares, where they are shrouded within the confines of this arable land, left by the people of days gone by. After agricultural intensification continued following the Second World War, what remained after further denuding was left to heal. Once industry retreated, the woods began to re-establish themselves in the newly formed edgelands which had been left behind. This derelict landscape soon became part of what we now call postmodern woodlands, where thousands of people help revitalise the environment to create opportunities for leisure, and social and economic development.

Tiddesley Woods, in this sense, has had a rich history. The woodland had once been a deer park, and was previously owned by Westminster Abbey. Historically, the woodland was actively managed by local people to provide timber, firewood and grazing, and in the 1950s, parts of the wood were felled and replanted with conifers by the Forestry Commission, which managed it for commercial purposes. Starting to remove the scrubland which had encroached its way in from the left-behind edgelands, the Forestry Commission had started to reinstate the native broad-leaved woodland which helps maintain the wildlife. Initially, it accomplished its goals, cutting back engulfing woodland until they became tight coppices to encourage new growth in different sectors. That was until Wychavon Council allowed building permission on the belt of the woods over five years ago. Unhindered by human interference, wildlife was left to flourish. Though but a memory, that was the Tiddesley Woods I had become accustomed to.

As I think back nostalgically on my walks through these woods, it seemed like the autumn leaves were catching fire in the late sun. I couldn't help but revel in the mysteries that surrounded me. My mother and our tricoloured basset hound in tow, it appeared there was a brand-new world waiting to be discovered. Here, I could act out my wildest fantasies: I could be a knight fighting monsters hidden in tight thickets of woodland, or a treasure hunter searching for the most precious of jewels. This was my hiding place, somewhere distant from society's grasp – somewhere I could break the conventions of having to grow up too fast.

As we walked further in, away from the busy main roads, the traffic would begin to taper to a background hum. The goldfinches and fieldfares would then go to work, their pleasant silvery twittering and melodic ticks ridding us of any remaining traces of nearby civilisation. Following the track of hardened mud which lay as our path, we would observe the meadow saffron, the Autumn queen in full bloom, hues of lilac and mauve creeping through the blankets of thistles and overgrown grasses. From one side to the other, it would take us at least forty minutes of uninterrupted trekking. After that, we would hit the box end gates where fields would slope out into the distance. From here, the River Avon could be seen on its convoluted journey through miles of grassy lands, towns, locks and weirs. Over the years, a long-distance footpath had been created from existing tracks, following the river in its entirety. Tourists and avid travellers can still be seen traversing the landscape regularly.

Our walks through this peaceful woodland became a regular weekend tradition. Sometimes, we would even take a packed lunch consisting of crustless ham sandwiches and plain crisps. Sitting on the nearest tree stumps, we would eat in silence and listen to the rustling of leaves in the mild summer breeze. Seasons would pass without a second glance, the scenery morphing and engulfing the previous periods of time which had been left behind. There were many signs of spring turning into summer, and autumn into winter. Dog's mercury in the spring with its serrate leaves would shrink back into the earth, leaving bald patches of sandy soil in its wake. In the winter, candlesnuff fungus would grow between the moist moss on tree stumps in place of devil's-bit, their violet capitula prominent before retreating and allowing the twisted and bent resemblance of stag's antlers to take its place. Of all the changes, one stood out more than the rest; that of the wild service tree, *Sorbus torminalis*. This indicator of ancient woodland sheds regularly, with its smooth grey bark peeling away in plates to reveal its darker brown underside. In May, the tree bears white clusters of budding flowers. These soon turn into dangling masses of russet ovoid pomes in mid- to late autumn, and can still be seen in winter. These changes, though subtle at first, become a distinguished part of nature. Alongside nature itself, the environment that I used to traverse in my childhood began to change too.

Becoming renowned as a Worcestershire Wildlife Trust reserve, more and more visitors would come to the woods in the hopes of spotting some of the rarer wildlife, including the noble chafer beetle, which lives and feeds on the rotting heartwood of trees. Coming with this wave of wildlife enthusiasts also came dog walkers, cyclists and tourists who would visit the town of Pershore as a holiday location. With this positivity and appeal, however, came a more uneasy truth.

Retreating from the town, the woods became a popular resort for teens at night, when the sun drowned in the horizon before fading completely. The area was relatively quiet, and was hidden beyond the codes of authority. This soon led to opportunities for littering. Our walks became shorter as we noticed used hypodermics cluttering the woodland bedding, alongside cans of beer and smashed glass protruding from thickets of wild rose and honeysuckle. It wasn't long before we stopped visiting completely, my adventures ceasing alongside them.

With time, everything changes. It may take months, if not years, but these changes will become noticeable. If some things feel remotely timeless, like the isolated areas of rural Britain, edgelands are anything but. Paul Farley and Michael Symmons Roberts in their book, *Edgelands*, describe them as such: 'Revisit an edgelands site you haven't seen for six months, and likely as not there will be a Victorian factory knocked down, a business park newly built, a section of waste ground cleared and landscaped, a pre-war warehouse abandoned and open to the elements'. They are not wrong. These changes were part of what I discovered when I revisited Tiddesley Woods, over ten years later.

The fields, once clustered in tightly packed groups near the edges of the woods had gone. In their place stood New Build homes, intricately designed yet crammed together like caged battery hens. Though still a distance from Tiddesley Woods itself, the views which once spanned miles of land were no more. With these homes came new visitors to the woods, and with this, more changes to the landscape. Notice boards had been placed at the main entrances, asking visitors to respect the following:

– Keep dogs on leads to avoid disturbing wildlife and please clean up after them.
– Keep to the marked trails and public rights of way.
– Take home any litter.
– Do not light fires and safely dispose of all sources of ignition.

We yearn for traces of our past woodland, the origins of our greenwoods, yet human interference hinders this. The signs, large enough for passers-by to take note of, had been mostly ignored. People would clean up after their dogs to an extent, their waste packed away in black bags. After this initial process though, the bags were left to hang precariously from tree branches, or simply stranded on the public rights of way. Litter including firelighters, glass, cans, and crisp packets had been left for so long that mosses, overgrown thickets of thorns and thistles had worked together to make human waste part of its natural habitat.

Though these intrusions have caused havoc to the natural environment, edgelands have been born from them. Asked to keep to the marked trails, people prefer wandering into the unknown, between tight crevices and through openings darkened by dense tree tops. From this, new paths have been made. Differing from the trails we see in our parks or wooded areas, these paths are made from lines of footfall, animal and human alike. Over the years, they have been worn into the ground, with some seeing them as scars upon nature. These are our desire paths, which lead you on a journey to concealed areas of the woods, and sometimes into open fields where nature crosses over. In the winter and early spring months, they become a slurry of wet mud that bonds to the undersides of shoes, and during the heat of summer they turn sooty and scorched.

Although these desire paths take us away from reality, allowing us to play out childhood memories from a forgotten past, the newly built civilisation surrounding the woods breaks you out from these casual daydreams. The delicate birdsong of marsh tits in the early spring, once known as the woodland's voice, can no longer outweigh the metallic screeches of industrial machines and the revving of car engines. To the end of the marked trails, where swathes of fields would dominate our vision, houses and main roads are in their stead. The fringes of society have started to push back against the community woodlands, to the point that they are entering their domain. The untouched space which had been left for property building on the edges of the woods had started to regain its stability. The waste ground, unearthed by loaders and excavators to reveal the undersides of the land, had been covered up by rotting deadwood which had fallen in the wintry winds just passed. Between this, a mixture of ruderal shrubs had formed, from evening primroses with their yolk and ivory petals to horsetail, their abrasive, ridged leaves spanning out into the other flora. Over time, these shrubs had knitted themselves together to create a protective layer for the soil, versatile enough to withstand the pressures of human force. Ebbing away from the communal woodland, these edgelands are rebellious and to an extent, feral. Their tame nature had been stripped from them, leading to an even stronger growth which fights against the borders of society.

Spending ten years away from somewhere I keep close to my heart when I think back to my childhood, these changes felt overwhelming. The neglect of nature gave a distinct antithesis to what my memory held dear; a place where beauty and perfection thrived now a little worse for wear, tired and in need of respite. I couldn't help but feel lost as I walked in silence, wildlife scarce and birds scattering from the trees as industrial machines whirred in their place. This had become a place where children could no longer play out their fantasies, too hazardous to be away from their parents' grasp. From all of this, though, a sliver of hope found its way in in the form of edgelands. Nature was reclaiming what had once been taken, the idea of woodland reverting back to its natural state a comforting one.

These new community woods have been designed to revive and regenerate the nature which once spanned miles of our countryside. They continue to spread their canopies over the landscape, closer into the breaches of civilisation. With this, it isn't long before the rural and urban begin their battle for domination, until one overshadows the other. This continues over time, and what they leave behind remains in the edgelands which surround our towns, villages and nature reserves. From this, young ecosystems are created, nature fighting back to help create biodiverse environments for wildlife. It is from this that we see the extent of what nature goes to, in order to help maintain the balance which is so sought after in our greenwoods. New roads may be built close to our rural areas, but one thing has been made clear: nature always finds a way to prevail.

The Collared Doves Are Drunk

Graham Jones

The collared doves are drunk!
Look, how they flutter and fall,
like Autumn leaves thrown back
and forth on an Autumn breeze,
or late night sailors
at the last port of call.
They have imbibed all day
on the fermented fruit
that has long been left to rot
around the rose-hip root.
The barn owl hovers
Viewing, with keen eyes,
the antics of the clerics
as they prance and dance
the requiem of the oblivious.
Silent and unseen, she swoops
and grabs and takes

Self-Portrait in a Landscape

Zachary Bos

I saw it painted on the pines and oaks.
– HD Thoreau

Maybe the stars look down and think of us
as silverfish resting on the top page
of a book whose words we cannot read, let
alone make sense of. To us, this book is
bread and board, meal and meadow, a vast hall
of linen, gilt leather and letter-shapes;
but seen from that celestial vantage point
the land is a book of annals telling
the memoir-story of nature itself --
the gold-limned calligraphic memory
of nature, the stage on which nature mums;
the murmuring of nature in its sleep
which is the book of the dream that nature
dreams to dream itself into mere being.

Lightning

Katie Ardern-Jones, aged 10

A flash of light spreading across darkness
dangerous as a shark's tooth
cutting the sky in half
as hot as the tip of a candle - bright as the sun
then dark like a black hole – quickly there
then gone
brightness clutching the earth in its bony hands

Katie Ardern-Jones

Entomological Beginnings

James McCulloch, aged 14

I've always loved the natural world, but recently I've begun to realise that I have a particular passion for entomology. My love of entomology has taught me not only to look up and around but also to look down, and examine any interesting looking leaf, rock or crevice. That is why when I step outdoors I will more frequently notice the straw-coloured veneer moths flitting up like angels from the grass by my feet than the blue tits that scatter from the nearby feeders.

During every excursion, be it into our small garden meadow or to the nature reserve down the road, I will invariably come across something I've never seen before. This is especially so when I visit a new area or reserve, as regularly they will possess a habitat I've never encountered before and therefore host multiple specialist species that would equally be new to me. This is less noticeable with the more adaptable avian or mammalian fauna, many species of which can survive in certain habitats such as woodlands or gardens regardless of the soil moisture level or the vegetation type. However this is not the same with many invertebrates, the diversity of which can vary from site to site depending on minute details such as whether a riverbed is mud, sand or pebble, or the availability of a single species of plant.

As I have developed what some could call entomological 'skills', I have learnt some of the places where unusual species or good numbers of invertebrates can be found. Therefore, whenever I'm out I'll always pay attention to the habitat or plants around me, and apply my knowledge of certain species, allowing me to check for their presence. As an example, I far more commonly come across holly bushes that do have the Agromyzid fly *Phytomyza ilicis* mining their leaves as opposed to ones that don't. However, until maybe a year or two ago, I would have been completely oblivious to their existence at all. I have also now learnt to examine any puffballs or earthballs I pass on my rambles for several beetles that are found exclusively in these fungi, like *Cryptophagus lycoperdi.*

Whenever I venture outside invertebrates are most of the time my main targets to see and I almost always see something that's completely new to me. Other than the direct searches such as for leaf mines and for species as specialist as *Cryptophagus lycoperdi*, I employ other techniques that turn up interesting invertebrates from multiple orders. My preferred way is definitely sweeping; I carry a sweep net with me

James McCulloch

Cockchafers

on nearly every outing. As well as interesting beetles and bugs I also turn up snails, hoverflies, moths and sometimes even tired damselflies! And one of the great things about sweeping is that even when surveying the same patch of plants, each sweep can have something different.

If I were to be asked, "What's your favourite insect order?" I doubt I could answer with much ease. Each order is unique and special in its own way. Odonata combine speed and ferocity; Siphonaptera can jump 100 times their height; and Orthoptera can "sing" purely using their legs and wings. However, if I were to pick a single order, I would probably choose the Coleoptera due to the sheer variety and number of species. Beetles make up 25 per cent of all animals with no less than 400,000 species and new species constantly being discovered. They range in size from *Dynastes hercules*, measuring 16.7cm, to *Scydosella musawasensis*, just 0.325mm long.

One of my favourite groups of beetles would be the Longhorns, one of the easiest groups to identify and they are generally rather attractive insects. I am lucky to have a few species I regularly come across in my garden, namely *Rutpela maculata* (Black and Yellow Longhorn), *Leptura quadrifasciata* (Four-banded Longhorn) and *Clytus arietis* (Wasp Beetle). All are black and yellow in colouration, with *Rutpela maculata* having black spots on a yellow elytra, *Leptura quadrifasciata* having yellow spots on black elytra and *Clytus arietis* having yellow stripes on black elytra. These are, noticeably, designed to mimic wasps despite being harmless. This type of mimicry is known as Batesian mimicry, and is when a non-harmful species mimics one that stings, is distasteful, or can otherwise hurt predators. *Clytus arietis* takes it a step beyond simply appearance – when threatened it even emits a wasp-like buzzing noise!

It's not just beetles that are excellent Batesian mimics, as I have discovered during my walks. I have come across many insects designed to mimic other, more dangerous insects, mostly wasps and bees. There are the hoverflies, such as *Helophilus pendulus* or *Chrysotoxum festivum*, and some harmless butterflies have evolved to mimic other toxic butterflies. And then there are those mimics, such as the Hornet mimic hoverfly *Volucella zonaria*, that mimic not to avoid predators but so that they can breed inside their hosts' nests unnoticed.

James McCulloch

Brown Hawker dragonfly

These are just a few of the examples of the incredible invertebrates I come across during my outings as a young entomologist. There are a plethora of other examples I have not yet mentioned, although I'm sure if I were to feature all of the impressive, bizarre and clever insects one could come across by just looking down a little more frequently, I would be able to fill at least a couple of volumes.

Four-banded Longhorn Beetle

James McCulloch

Alone in the Wild

Lynn Parr

The sea is a silk scarf; supine. Holly green and glossy, barely rising and falling with the merest breath of wind. The boat slips past the craggy fingertip of the peninsula, its familiar cottages and tracks becoming different, unknown when viewed from the sea. The swells begin to lift, mirroring the shape of the mountains beyond.

Then we are out beyond the embrace of the land – and suddenly, we are alone and tiny in the vast Atlantic, tossed about like a feather in a gale. The boat lifts on a crest, then plunges, a wall of deep green rising up to overlook us, blocking out the land that already seems so far away and fading into mist.

Puffins paddle madly by in mid-air as if afraid they will fall if they stop flapping. Pyroclastic gannets streak into the water all around, or skim through the skin of a wave, tango-ing with their shadows. Guillemots, black guillemots and razorbills raft by; rain begins to pit the dark, oily water. And all around, as far as we can see, white fingers grip the edges of waves and tip them up, as if things are peering at us from the deep, or trying to climb out.

Spray-drenched and wind-blasted, we stare into the mist to find a familiar shape; a handhold of land to steady us; something solid to which we can cling so we are not whirled away on the wind and current. A safe harbour for our souls. And eventually, a great grey eminence arises from the sea, stitching the water to the clouds. Skellig Michael, cathedral of the Atlantic.

As the boat draws near, we can smell the fishy aroma of its guano-green neighbour, screaming with birds. And there are the rock-hewn steps, winding up the vertical wall, to the old monastic beehive cells somewhere up in the clouds.

There's something about wild and perilous places that resonates with our core. We have always sought wilderness for spiritual focus, far from the distractions of the everyday; but such places also promise solitude and, perhaps, the challenge of self-denial and surviving somewhere difficult. The monks who colonized Skellig Michael off the west coast of Ireland were not the first people to struggle up its sheer walls; to live on its wind-blasted crown. For the name they gave this oceanic rock – as with all the hilltop and mountain religious sites in the Celtic regions – dedicated it to the great archangel charged with driving out demons: demons they believed were called by pagan worship at those sites, which had been considered sacred for centuries. But why did Neolithic and Bronze Age people choose such inaccessible places to connect with their deities? Did the sheer challenge of getting there and surviving form part of their spiritual growth? Or did they seek wilderness like people do today: for the quiet of spiritual connection they can't find in a bustling world? Hoping to find a kinship with wild creatures they can't find with other people? Or merely the self-satisfaction of overcoming the vast, uncaring otherness of Nature and 'taming' it, as Western pioneers have done throughout the ages?

Can modern humans really go back to belonging in the wild? Even the last hunter-gatherer tribes – the "Uncontacted" – still live in groups with others. Few people live completely alone in the wilderness without some kind of tether to the human world, whether tinned food or satellite phone. And alone you still have to live with yourself: you have to be strong to overcome the creeping nightmares of the past and imagined terrors of the present that lurk in our darkest corners.

Perhaps that fear of the Wild – for facing yourself; trusting yourself – accounts for the shrinking wilderness areas of the world. Human ingenuity has buffered us all with gadgets, electronic devices and layers of lies convincing us we need what others have; that we are incomplete and somehow inadequate without the constant bragging and oneupmanship with others. Fuelling our natural insecurities; reaffirming our feelings of worthlessness with insidious bullying whispers: *Buy this; do that.* Telling us we can't survive without stuff; without others. Making us afraid to try.

Yet we know wilderness heals. Just getting away from the stress of day-to-day living by being alone in a wild place can refresh your spirit. We don't need to struggle to survive on windswept pinnacles to feel a connection with the natural world; we don't need to revert to hunter-gathering deep in a jungle. We know that sharing your life with a pet or feeding the birds brings rewards far beyond owning a human-made article. Simply working in a garden or walking in the countryside can renew your armour against modern life.

The Wild is all around us: from lichen quilting a wall to a toadstool thrusting through tarmac; a bumblebee humming along a windowbox to a red kite polishing the sky. Wilderness can be perilous, yes: but also forgiving. And it belongs to all of us. Whether you seek spiritual answers or just peace of mind, take a moment to turn off that smartphone; stop and focus. The Wild is out there: and it's calling.

Gannet-covered Little Skellig with Skellig Michael beyond.
Lynn Parr

Contributors

John Burroughs (1837-1921) was an acclaimed author living in the Hudson Valley region of the USA. He wrote hundreds of articles, essays and books, creating the nature essay tradition still followed today. He travelled in the wilderness with celebrated figures such as Theodore Roosevelt, Walt Whitman and John Muir, and helped establish the conservation movement by bringing the natural world to his readers. 'Bird Song' appeared in his book *Ways of Nature*, 1905. www.johnburroughsassociation.org

Lynne Caddick, originally from Yorkshire, currently lives close to the Sandstone Trail, Cheshire. She belongs to the Shrewsbury Stanza poetry group and attends the Nantwich Speakeasy and Whitchurch BookShop poetry events.

Finola Scott's poems have been widely published in anthologies and magazines including The Ofi Press, *Obsessed with Pipework*, *The Lake*, *And Other Poems*, and *Clear Poetry*. Through poetry she tries to understand and explain the places where she finds herself and what she observes in the world. A Glaswegian, she describes herself as a "Slam-winning granny".

Cliff Wright draws, illustrates, writes and sculpts his way through life and teaches drawing-based workshops under the name of Nature of Seeing, in which he helps reveal participants' authentic creativity and connections to wild nature. He is best known for his illustrations on the covers of the original Harry Potter books, and his work has been published in the UK and abroad for countless children's books, magazines, greetings cards, posters, advertising, and so on. Most of the images in this Curlew essay were taken by Cliff's infrared motion detecting camera that the wildlife has become used to over time. www.cliffwright.co.uk

Pat Edwards is a writer, teacher and performer living in the countryside in Mid Wales, which inspires her poetry. She has been widely published online and runs Verbatim poetry open mic nights. She uses the natural world in her poetry as a metaphor for events and feelings. Pat is the curator of Welshpool Poetry Festival.

Alison Brackenbury published her first collection, *Dreams of Power*, with Carcanet in 1981. It was a Poetry Book Society Recommendation and won an Eric Gregory Award. Since then, she has published eight more collections, won a Cholmondeley Award (for the whole of her work) and had her work broadcast regularly on BBC Radio 3 and BBC Radio 4. Her latest collection, *Skies* (Carcanet, 2016), was featured on 'Front Row', on BBC Radio 4, and in the UK national press. *Skies* was chosen by *The Observer* as one of its Poetry Books of the Year. www.alisonbrackenbury.co.uk

Rachel Burns is a poet and playwright living in Durham, England. Her poems have been published in various UK literary magazines, and have been shortlisted in competitions in *Mslexia*, *Writers' & Artists' Yearbook* and The Keats-Shelley Poetry Prize 2017.

Maggie Mackay, a recent Manchester Metropolitan University MA Poetry graduate, has work in a range of publications including *Atrium* and *Amaryllis*. Her poem 'How to Distil a Guid Scotch Malt' was nominated for The Forward Prize, Best Single Poem, 2017.
Jonathan Trim is an artist living in Leigh-on-Sea, Essex. The Thames Estuary has always

been an important presence in his life – he loves the rhythms and seasons, and the ever-changing light. It is no accident then, that as a painter, it has become a constant theme for him. His work is available from a large number of galleries in the UK and from his studio. www.jonathantrim.com

Kitty Coles lives in Surrey, and her poems have been widely published in magazines and anthologies. She was one of the two winners of the Indigo Dreams Pamphlet Prize 2016, and her debut pamphlet, *Seal Wife*, was published in September 2017. www.kittyrcoles.com

David Crews lives in New Jersey, USA, and is author of the poetry collections *High Peaks* (RA Press, 2015) and *Circadian Rhythm* (Paulinskill Poetry Project, 2014). New poems and essays are forthcoming or recent in *Canary*, *Tiferet*, *Lime Hawk*, *Bird's Thumb*, *Stoneboat*, *Flightpath*, *Platform Review*, and others. He is the editor of *The Stillwater Review*. www.davidcrewspoetry.com

Aziz Dixon lives in the Rossendale Valley, Lancashire, and draws on local Pennine and Welsh landscapes and life experiences for his poetry. He has been published in various publications, inclusing *Pennine Ink*, *Irwell Inkwell*, *Algebra of Owls*, *Grapevine*, *Moon Magazine*, *Panoply* and *Perspectives*.. He launched his latest collection, *Poet Emerging*, with a reading at the Burnley Literary Festival 2016 and on Radio Lancashire, England.

Tee Francis is a therapeutic writing facilitator, based in Dorset. She believes that our natural environment is an essential part of the therapeutic journey. Nature not only inspires us, it promotes acceptance, sanctuary and a sense of wholeness.

Jane Burn is an artist and writer based in the UK's North East. Her poems have been featured in magazines such as *The Rialto*, *Under The Radar*, *Butcher's Dog*, *Iota Poetry*, *And Other Poems*, *The Black Light Engine Room* and many more, as well as in anthologies from the Emma Press, Beautiful Dragons, Poetry Box, Emergency Poet and Kind of a Hurricane Press. Her pamphlets include *Fat Around the Middle*, (Talking Pen) and *Tongues of Fire* (BLER Press). Her first full collection, *nothing more to it than bubbles* was published by Indigo Dreams. She also established the poetry site The Fat Damsel. She was longlisted in the 2014 and 2016 National Poetry Competition, commended and highly commended in the Yorkmix 2014 and 2015, and won the inaugural Northern Writes Poetry Competition in 2017.

Steve Harrison lives in Shropshire in the shadow of The Wrekin. His work has been published by charities, the Wenlock Poetry Festival, the Ledbury Poetry Physic Garden and the two Emergency Poet collections, and will appear in the next *Wetherspoons Magazine*. He regularly performs across the Midlands and won the Ledbury Poetry Festival Slam in 2014.

Audrey Ardern-Jones lives in Surrey and is currently a student with Matthew Caley at the Poetry School. She has been published in various magazines and anthologies. She reads poetry to sick children in the hospital where she is a volunteer and helps with artwork.

Deborah Vass is a painter and printmaker who lives on the borders of Norfolk and

Suffolk. Her artwork is inspired by the birds, plants and wildlife of her garden and the countryside of the local fens, where she sketches and records the changes of the seasons. www.deborahvass.com

Carolyn Martin lives in Oregon, USA. From English teacher to management trainer to retiree, she has journeyed from New Jersey to Oregon to discover Douglas firs, months of rain, and perfect summers. Her poems and book reviews have appeared in publications throughout North America and the UK, including *Stirring*, *CALYX*, *Persimmon Tree*, *How Higher Education Feels* (Sense), and *Antiphon*. Her third collection, *Thin Places*, was released by Kelsay Books in 2017. Since the only poem she wrote in high school was red-penciled "extremely maudlin," Carolyn is amazed she has continued to write.

Fred Montague earned a PhD in vertebrate ecology from Purdue University in 1975 and taught wildlife ecology and environmental science at Purdue from 1975 until 1992. In 1993 he accepted a position in the Biology Department at the University of Utah teaching wildlife ecology, environmental science, literature of ecology, and principles of organic gardening. He retired in 2010 and is currently Professor (Lecturer) Emeritus. In addition to university teaching, Fred has also had a parallel career as a wildlife artist. Initially, he created illustrations for his wildlife work, and gradually the art became another way to teach. His work is collected throughout the United States and in several other countries. www.mountainbearink.com

Ram Nag lives in Mumbai, India, and is moved by the beauty of nature. He loves life and explores the material, philosophical and spiritual aspects of life through his poems. He believes that there is more to life than 'earning, acquiring and losing'. He believes that the natural state of man is joy, and all our efforts to acquire and keep pace with others make us lose our joy. He hopes to capture the beauty of life through his poems, which have been published by Page & Spine and *Illumen*. His poem 'One or two' received an Honorable Mention in the Rhyming Riddles Contest organized by The Society of Classical Poets.

Holly-Elizabeth Toney lives in Pershore, Worcestershire. Her work has been published in the University of Worcester's Creative and Professional Writing magazine, *The Sabrina*. Her inspiration for 'Edgelands of Tiddesley Woods' came from Paul Farley and Michael Symmons Robert's book, *Edgelands* (Jonathan Cape, 2011), as well as walks in local wildlife reserves. This inspiration was further fuelled by an interest in various environmental and contemporary issues.

Graham Jones lives in Norfolk but spent a happy childhood roaming the countryside of North Wales. From that rich tapestry developed his love of writing and singing. Many of his poems have appeared in magazines and poetry collections, and he has organised poetry festivals and a national poetry competition. He loves to visit poetry groups for readings, and enjoys talking about poetry in schools and other groups. Graham believes everyone has a poem to write, and loves helping individuals draw out their own particular muse.

Zachary Bos studied poetry in the Boston University MFA program. His poetry has appeared in journals including *Public Pool*, *Written River*, and *Fallujah*, and was long-listed for the 2017 Disquiet Poetry Prize. He is editor of *Hawk & Whippoorwill* journal, and publisher of *The New England Review of Books*. @zakbos.

Katie Ardern-Jones lives in the New Forest. She loves poetry, nature and sport. She won the Portswood Library under-16 centenary writing competition in 2015 – 'What my library means to me' – with a poem.

James McCulloch, from West Sussex, has a particular passion for the world's smaller fauna. He loves being out-and-about searching for wildlife, particularly invertebrates, whenever he has the opportunity. He is a trainee bird ringer, an active member of ispotnature.org, and does moth trapping and Longworth mammal trapping to record local nature. James was the winner of the Gilbert White Youth Award in 2015. His blog, Only Natural, can be found at www.jiainmac.wordpress.com.

Lynn Parr is a writer and artist living in West Wales. Her books and articles have been published in the UK, USA and Ireland. She has edited international magazines and books, and taught poetry, creative writing and ecology in schools and universities. Her children's novel, *Dangerous Secrets!*, and her new book of nature essays, *Still Waters: Fragments of Nature & Place*, were published by Southwind Books. www.lynnparr.co.uk

Writing for
The Curlew

The Curlew invites writers to contribute original, thought-provoking essays, poems and short stories with a connection to the natural world. Emerging writers and artists are just as welcome as well-known ones.

Non-fiction narratives and short stories should be less than 3,000 words; poems no more than two A4 typed pages. An exception is the Classic Essay, for which suggestions are welcome.

Illustrations and photographs are also required. They should print well in black and white. Please send low-resolution images at first.

Writers under 16 are invited to submit for the Sanderlings section.

All work must be original. Previously published work is acceptable as long as the author holds the copyright.

There is no payment for contributions as *The Curlew* is a non-profit venture, supporting conservation projects around the world.

Send email queries to info@the-curlew.com. Please be patient while awaiting a response. The editor's decision is final.

Please see the website, www.the-curlew.com, for more detailed guidelines on content and style.